# 1 MONTH OF
# FREE
# READING

at

## www.ForgottenBooks.com

By purchasing this book you are eligible for one month membership to ForgottenBooks.com, giving you unlimited access to our entire collection of over 1,000,000 titles via our web site and mobile apps.

To claim your free month visit:

www.forgottenbooks.com/free230747

ISBN 978-0-483-78199-3
PIBN 10230747

# DALMAQUA

### A Legend of Aowasting Lake
### Near Lake Minnewaska
### Shawangunk Mountains, New York

BY

## JARED BARHITE, Ph.D.

*Superintendent of Schools, West New York, N. J.*

---

### THE INDIANS

In legend and in names they live,
   By lake and stream and mountain wild;
Seldom a thought to them we'd give,
   Were these reminders but despoiled.
Their forms have faded from the land,
   Their songs unheard upon the shore,
They sleep in death on every hand,
   Their war-whoops wild are heard no more.

---

## EDUCATIONAL PUBLISHING COMPANY
### BOSTON
NEW YORK    CHICAGO    SAN FRANCISCO

# EXPLANATORY NOTE

After the discovery of the Hudson River by the Dutch in 1609, the States-General of Holland granted, in 1614, to the New Netherland Company certain rights "to visit, navigate, and use" the lands discovered.

In the Spring of 1615, a party of Dutch traders landed at Ponckhockie, now the southeasterly part of the city of Kingston, N. Y., built a fort, and established a trading post there, calling it Rondout.

The traders were received by the Indians with great hospitality mingled with awe. Corn and game were given the settlers, hoping thereby to secure their friendship and protection. Encroachments were soon made upon the possessions of the Indians and they began to defend their rights by force and stratagem. Governor Kieft, in 1643, determined to exterminate the Indians in the region of the Catskills and the Shawangunk Mountains, and made war upon them for that purpose. Many Indians were killed and many captives taken during this war, but, failing to carry out his purpose of extermination, he deported the captives to Curacoa, an island belonging to the Dutch, situated in the Southern West Indies, where they were consigned to slavery. Many of the Indian captives died there from the inhospitable climate and from the severe servitude to which they were subjected. This war was carried on for a number of years, although intercourse with the Indians was at no time fully suspended.

In the fall of 1659, a party of Indians had been husking corn for Thomas Chambers, a prominent citizen and an official in the settlement of Ponckhockie, when they were attacked by the whites and eight of their number killed. Their only offence was in becoming drunk and somewhat noisy among themselves, from rum furnished by Chambers, as partial payment for services. This was at evening after the regular labor of the day had ended. Evert Pels, the chief official (schapen) permitted the massacre to take place, although it is not certain that he participated in it directly. The survivors and their friends fled to Aowasting Lake, some thirty miles to the westward, carrying their dead companions with them.

This lake, situated in the Shawangunk Mountains, was the rendezvous for the Indians, and within three days a force of five hundred assembled there to avenge the death of their eight companions.

About a week after the Ponckhockie massacre, the Indians, after marching by night along the valley of the Wallkill and sleeping by day upon its wooded banks, fell upon the citizens of Ponckhockie and killed many, taking also some captives. Among the latter was Petrus Pels, a son of Evert Pels, who was largely responsible for the massacre. The attack lasted about three weeks, from which great destruction of property and much cruelty ensued.

The Indians then returned to Aowasting Lake, taking with them the captives and trophies. Young Pels was adopted and afterwards married Dalmaqua, the daughter of Nakosing, who had been killed in the massacre.

Dalmaqua's mother died some fifteen years before this marriage and during the war with Governor Kieft, whether from violence or not, is not known.

Ondoris, Nakosing's brother, took care of Dalmaqua after the death of her father.

A brother of Ondoris and Nakosing was killed in war with Governor Kieft about the time of the death of Dalmaqua's mother.

Aowasting Lake was the home of Ondoris, Nakosing, and Dalmaqua, the latter knowing no other home. Here Petrus Pels met Dalmaqua and married her.

Within a sharp angle formed by two high cliffs, a little to the southeast of Aowasting Lake, and not far from its borders, among the most picturesque scenes of the Shawangunks, is a huge granite block, lying among hundreds of smaller ones, thrown from the cliffs by convulsed Nature, upon which are the features of a man in sphinx-like repose, looking southward over the valley of the Wallkill. The block is somewhat elevated above its fellows and lies at an angle of about sixty-five degrees. A crown rests upon its head.

Legend says that upon the refusal of Petrus Pels to return to his home and kindred, at Kingston, when importuned to do so by emissary scouts, he was shot and killed by whites, and that Dalmaqua, after long and patient labor, carved his features upon the rock to perpetuate the memory of her devoted husband, and to teach her son the virtues and heroism of his father.

Lake Aowasting, near Lake Minnewaska, is a beautiful body of water some two miles in length, at an elevation of more than two thousand feet above the sea level. These lakes are in a wild, picturesque region, abounding in cliffs, cascades, ravines, and glacier-polished rocks. Their shores are rocky and fringed with fir, pine, hemlock, balsam, and deciduous trees of many kinds. The cliffs, near the shores, are in some places, nearly perpendicular and rise to great heights. The Wallkill and the Rondout streams unite some five or six miles above Ponckhockie and form an estuary of much beauty and great commercial value. Aowasting means place of crossing and resting. Ponckhockie means place for canoes. Minnewaska means frozen water.

Lake Minnewaska is a well known and popular summer resort near Lake Aowasting. The elevation, vegetation, and environments of these lakes are conducive to health and enjoyment. The lover of nature can here find her in her most romantic and attractive aspects, and within a region healthful in surroundings, easily accessible from great cities, and abounding in legend and romance most fascinating and grand.

THE ONLY HOUSE ON THE SHORE OF AOWASTING LAKE, NEAR OUTLET OF LAKE

# DALMAQUA

*The Coming of the Dutch in* 1615

'Twas time when the leaf was returning
And the brown was exchanging for green;
When the sun warmed Nature to action,
In the springtime of sixteen-fifteen,
On a mission of commerce and daring,
The Dutch, with sails gaily drest,
Sped away from the Lowlands of Holland
To the Netherlands of the West.

They entered the land of Algonquins,
Where broad Hudson flows in a bed,
Carved thro' the rugged mountains,
Whose crown, on each separate head,
Proclaims it a land of Freedom,
Where bondage shall be unknown;
Where the wigwam and the castle
Are the owner's rightful throne.

Thirty leagues to northward, and away
From the green islands at the sea,
Is a peaceful harbor, broad and deep,
Whose supreme tranquillity
Bid weary strangers seek repose
And commerce on its shore,
Where Wallkill and the Rondout join
And into the Hudson pour.

The canoes were moored at Ponckhockie,
Away from the rushing tide,
The Indians, at noonday, reposing
The peaceful river beside;
The sun in its vernal splendor,
Shone brightly on mountain and shore,
When came there a strange apparition,
Unknown in that land before.

Its wings were like drifts of winter
Advancing upon the wave;
It moved toward their place of resting
Though no sign of life it gave;
It seemed like a spirit advancing
From regions of unknown space,
And bearing away for Ponckhockie
To secure an abiding place.

All eyes were turned toward the vision
That came on the breath of the wind;
Grim terror seizéd the warriors
Though bravest of their kind;
The women fled in terror
To the hills for a safe retreat;
While tremblingly the chieftains
Prepared the unknown to meet.

Instinctive council brief was held,
Whether to fight, or appease
With offerings of choicest gifts,
Upon their bended knees;
Or betake themselves to the mountains,
Or submit to the stranger band
As a messenger of the Manitou,
Sent from the spirit land.

The grass their arrows soon concealed,
Their spears were laid aside,
Their hands were stretched to the phantom
          crew
That on the winds could ride;
They welcomed them as from above,
From the Father Manitou;
They vied in valor and in chase
To prove their friendship true.

## Desolation Caused by Avarice

Thus four and forty years were passed,
Since, on this peaceful shore,
The pale-face planted here his home
And reaped his yearly store;
But Avarice, the white man's bane,
Had sown the seeds of woe,
Had robbed of lands and corn and grain,
Laid many a red man low.

Man's greed for gold, for land, for power,
Has strewn the earth with woe and pain,
Spread carnage o'er earth's fairest fields,
Where myriad millions have been slain
To build for Mammon, Pomp, and Pride,
An altar, whereat he may bring
The victims, he, self-deified,
Would deem a sacred offering.

No human wail of deep distress —
No pleading for one's land and home
Can touch a chord in Avarice's breast
When he insatiate has become;
His ears are deaf, his eyes are blind,
He heeds no plaintive, pleading cry,
But dulled by cruel selfishness,
He laughs at victim's agony.

A weakling brother he will slay —
From impotence advantage wrest,
And justify such robbery
As a survival of the best;
Transforming thus, men into beasts
To batten on the spoils, that come
From blighted hopes and agonies
That hover 'round a ruined home.

Deaf are his ears, all senses dulled,
By eagerness in his pursuit
Of human prey which may, perchance,
Increase his pride or pomp or boot;
His brother's face he would eclipse
Behind the greed that lures him on,
Until all trace of tenderness
And acts of manliness are gone.

The pearly gates of heaven he'd seize,
Its jasper walls, filch for his own,
And tear the golden tinselry
From off the great celestial throne;
Feel no compunction for the deed,
No sting of conscience keenly feel,
Nor blanch to read, then, Sinai's law
To Moses given, "Thou shalt not steal."

With iron hand and marble heart,
With jaws agape on woes to feed,
He forfeits honor, truth, and right
As sacrifices to his greed;
Forgetful that a time shall come,
When he must lay his all aside,
To cross the Stygian pool to meet
The Master he has long defied.

### The Massacre and Flight

September brought its carnival
Of blood and death and woe,
When, of the red men, eight were slain
By shot and sword and blow,
At Thomas Chambers' husking bee,
When fiery draughts were given
To serve for wages they had earned,
Before that fatal even.

Ten leagues to westward fled their friends,
Where giant cliffs and dark ravine
Concealed their presence from the foe,
And formed great barriers between.
Here gathered all the mighty men,
From north and south and east and west,
To counsel of the impending storm,
And plan such action as seemed best.

## Ondoris' Musings

Ondoris broods o'er brothers' fall
By hand of avaricious Kieft;
On Dalmaqua, his brother's child —
A worthy offspring of the chief —
Whose birth-date is coequal with
Her mother's sad and early death;
Her home there in the wilderness,
Now motherless and fatherless;

Recalls the story of their wrongs,
And points to mound not far away,
Where fifteen years before, he laid
His brother's form to meet decay.
Now Dalmaqua's loved father falls
Beneath the stroke of bloody men
Whose avarice has led them on
To slaughter and rapine again.

He sits beside his humble tent
In pensive mood, in silence stern,
And gazes on the burial mound
That shields two fallen brothers' urn;
His quivering lip, his dewy eye
Betray his heart's deep agony;
Unspoken is his deep despair —
No sound save half-suppresséd sigh

That speaks a language far too deep
To be translated, but by him
Who through experience has felt
The selfsame arrows, sharp and grim.
No words can fathom stricken soul
Bowed down in sorrow and distress
Through death of kindred, at the hand
Of greed's envenomed bitterness.

The sighing wind that drives the clouds
Across the horn of dripping moon,
Presaging wild September's storms
And boding frost-king's reign full soon,
Draws not his eye from nearby grave
That shields two brothers' forms laid low
By pale-faced stranger from afar,
Who dealt the fatal, murd'rous blow.

The evening's glorious western sky
All crimsoned with the dying day,
'The myriad-insect minstrelsy
That holds nocturnal revelry,
The breeze that sings at equinox
Among the pines, æolian strain,
Were but reminders of those days
On which his brothers had been slain.

Ensanguined clouds in distant west
Bespoke of kinsmen's blood that flowed;
The insect-hum and sighing blast
Were requiems at death's abode.
And, as the night her mantle cast
Upon the lake and cliff and wood,
A solemn stillness reigned supreme
And made intense the solitude.

### Alone

The anguish of a stricken soul
That lives though life has lost its charm,
That feels no joy to cheer its way,
And heeds no tocsin of alarm,
Is only known to those whose lives
Have lost that sweet companionship
That melts the dross from human souls,
And gives consoling inborn bliss

Through faith and trust and love supreme,
Made sacred by some mutual cause
Which binds by ties of brotherhood
As strong as God's unerring laws,
Casting aside Hope's radiant bow,
Asks not from sorrow a reprieve,
But finds an inward legacy
Of sweet enjoyment, still to grieve.

When anchors of life's voyage are gone,
To voyager, vain is vital breath,
For wounded heart that still lives on,
Oft suffers anguish worse than death;
And brightest things that God e'er made
Are veiled to such by somber cloud
On which dire portent is displayed,
And boding mists heaven's joys enshroud.

When life has lost the golden link
That binds it to a kindred heart,
And deep Despair holds revelry
With all his agony and smart,
The tension of the mind must break
Unless the Master's hand shall stay
The current of destruction's power
And turn aside its agony.

Ondoris lifts his fallen eye,
His spirit seems anew aflame,
He cries aloud for Justice's aid,
Calls Dalmaqua's dear father's name;
Then pouring all his plea to Him
Who wards away the battle stroke,
In orison to Spirit Great,
These words in reverence he spoke:

FROM LEDGE NEAR HOUSE, LOOKING UP LAKE AOWASTING

## *Ondoris' Orison*

"Great Manitou, who reigns above,
And heeds His children's plaintive cry,
Guard thou our tents, our fields, our lakes,
Nor let our sons and brothers die;
Stretch forth the curtain of the cloud
And veil our kinsmen from the foe
Whose thunders fill our hearts with fear,
And lifeless lay our brothers low.

"From the dark cloud that hovers 'round
The head of Shawangunk's highest peak,
In accents stern, majestic, firm,
Great Spirit, now in thunders speak
And teach the pale-faced men of war
That we are children of the same
Almighty hand that led them forth,
And equal heritage we claim.

"This land is heritage bequeathed
By you to children of this wild,
Here we have dwelt, through countless moons,
And kept its soil pure, undefiled,
Till summoned by our kinsmen's fall,
We stood upon the mountain side
And hurled defiance at our foes
Until our brave defenders died.

"Then, then like hunted beasts we fled
To cave and rock and secret den,
And let concealment aid our cause
Till we might venture forth again.
Each rock and tree, each cliff and glen,
Was brother with an outstretched arm,
To guard us in our weakness when
We fled from death in wild alarm.

"These rocks, though flinty to our touch,
Are soft, compared to greed's embrace;
These caves, though dark and desolate,
More cheering than abiding place
'Mong stranger bands, whose hands purloined
The heritage our fathers gave,
And left our only legacy —
The sweet protection of a grave.

"Three days have passed since we beheld
Our brothers slain without a cause,
Two days have gathered in this wild
Our kinsmen true to tribal laws;
To-morrow guide our feet aright.
Five hundred warriors, strong and brave,
Have burned their incense in the field
Beside my murdered brother's grave.

"At war-dance we have met again,
Around its fires our songs were sung,
Arrows were plumed and rightly poised,
Our bows with proper tension strung,
And, in each breast of warrior true,
There burns a strong, intense desire
To free our land from those who quench
Our life-blood and our wigwam fire.

"Could Peace and Justice but unite,
And Avarice be held in chain,
Our land would ample fruitage bear,
Our sons and brothers, be not slain.
But you, Great Spirit, gave to us
This land as primal heritage,
And thus, committed to our trust,
We must in its defense engage."

### The War-Dance

Brave Minquas and lithe Minnesinks
By Aowasting's rockbound shore;
While Nanticokes and Delawares
Lake Minnewaska stand before.
From every clan, from every tribe —
War-on-a-wan-kings from the east,
And the Wa-war-sings from the west,
Were gathered at the war-dance feast.

The cliffs that Minnewaska fringe
Re-echoed Aowasting's song,
And Aowasting's warwhoops rang
The Shawangunk's rugged rocks among,
Till valley, lake, and cliff, and wood
Were resonant with shout and yell,
And dance-fires cast their lurid lights
Like flames escaped from nether hell.

The stars of heaven but dimly shone,
And mirrored clouds on lake did rest,
While phantom fires hung in the air
Suspended o'er the mountain crest,
Presaging scenes of toil and strife,
But daunting not the purpose high,
Of men who sought to shield their homes,
Or in their efforts nobly die.

The baying wolves, from ledge to ledge,
In prophecy of strife and war,
Sent tidings on the wings of winds
To hungry comrades near and far,
While answering bayings from the vale,
Seemed echoings from cliffs full nigh,
Till re-reverberations filled
The trembling air and boding sky.

Five hundred chosen men there were,
The young, the brave, the swift, the strong,
All gathered round the fires at night
To join in sacred dance and song,
While aged fathers pensive stood,
All pleading the Great Manitou
To turn aside the pale-face's stroke,
But guide aright the avenging blow.

### The March Toward Ponckhockie

Along the Shawangunk's southern side,
Through woods that skirt the stream below,
Till from the north it meets its kin
And joins the Rondout in its flow,
In stealthy silence sped they on
Beneath the waning harvest moon,
Till from the east the day-god came,
Dispelling darkness all too soon.

Soft sylvan shades sweet silence held,
Save song of some sequestered bird
Whose dirge to dying summer's sun,
Within a mottled copse was heard.
The winds were hushed, the stream subdued,
And falling leaf by breeze unswayed,
Descended gently to the sward,
Whereon nocturnal fairies played,

Bright crimsoned leaves the light obscured
And carpeted the turf below,
While stately pines stood sentinels
To guard autumnal maples' glow.
Beside the stream that found its way
'Mong tangled briars, vines, and wood,
In one grand galaxy, there grew
Wild asters and bright goldenrod.

Her regal charms here Nature spread,
Then left her votaries to admire;
Extended here her magic hand
To lift her devotees still higher,
And place them on an eminence
Where grace and beauty intertwine
To spread heaven's curtain, and reveal
The handiwork of the Divine.

Here sentineled Ondoris slept
The broken sleep which warriors know,
Before the conflict has begun,
And face to face have met the foe.
In dreams he sees the vanquishéd,
And hears their agonizing plea
For mercy, from the hands of those
Whose friends were slain at Ponckhockie.

He sees his brother stricken down
Beneath the slaughtering hand of men
Who led him into evil ways,
But turned him not toward right again;
And as the scene of horror came
In force across his slumber-thought,
His brow was knit, his hand fast clinched
Upon the dream-born murderer's throat;

And summoning his every power,
He grappled fiercely with the foe
Who had betrayed his kinsmen dear,
And laid his friends and brothers low;
And, as the conflict, fierce, supreme,
Waxed warmer, deadlier than before,
His frame convulsed, eyes opened wide,
And seemingly life was no more.

The sun o'er Shawangunk's western peaks
Had half concealed its autumn glow,
The mists were rising in the vale
Where Wallkill's sluggish waters flow,
When summons came once more to move
Toward Ponckhockie's blood-stainéd hills.
Ondoris then his dream relates,
Till nerve of every warrior thrills,

To fight on field, as he in dreams
Had fought in Wallkill's silent wood,
Prepared to vindicate their cause
Or shed the last drop of his blood.
Their hope of home, of friends, of life,
Upon this triumph seemed to rest,
And stern resolve to conquer foes
Was fixed in every warrior's breast.

When all we love on earth is gone
And Hope departs on sable wing,
When wreckage from life's plan floats by
And leaves no plank to which to cling,
Then Gaunt Despair will seize the soul,
Unless the God of earth and sky
Shall rouse some latent power within
And lend it heaven-born energy.

Alone, our hands too feeble are
To stem life's seething, hungry tide,
In vain we buffet with the world,
Unless, with greater strength allied,
We nerve the arm and soothe the soul,
By intercourse with hidden power,
Whose ministry sufficient is
To cheer in life's despairing hour.

There dwells in man an occult power
Whose silent force must need combine
The energies of human will
With guidance from a hand divine,
And blend in unison the strength
That both can offer, to assuage
The buffetings and sorrowings,
That form, in part, life's heritage.

He lives for naught, who has not felt
The strength that comes from intercourse
With that mysterious, wondrous charm
That claims earth's Maker as its source.
Who feels no fires from kindling torch
That warms, illumes, and guides his way,
Held in a hand whose guidance turns
His darkest night to noontide day.

Ondoris seemed himself again;
His eye, a brighter lustre wore;
His step was firm, his sinews strong,
As he, along the Wallkill's shore,
And 'twixt its margin, and the rocks
That towering hang on northern side,
Strode with a purpose fixed and firm,
As one who would not be defied.

A brother's blood avenged must be;
The maiden's prayer, around the fire,
Has nerved his hand to do her will
And'slay the murderer of her sire.
In this one act, for her alone,
No barrier must now impede,
For Justice calls on him aloud,
And he must shrink not from the deed.

### Avenging the Massacre

Again Ponckhockie's shores appear
Beneath the stars of early night,
And slaughter reigns on every side
As hand to hand the foemen fight.
'Mid dead and dying, captives, too,
Are some who but five days before
Had revelled in the murderous raid
And drenched those hills in redmen's gore.

Among the captives was a youth,
A son of one who wielded power
But stayed not the destroying hand,
Upon that dread nocturnal hour,
When Dalmaqua's departed sire —
A brother of Ondoris brave —
Was slaughtered in ignoble strife
And laid in Aowasting's grave.

Full twenty suns had sunk behind
The hills where dead Nakosing slept,
And twenty moons had gilt the waves
Where nightly Dalmaqua had wept,
When back the weary warriors came;
But not in numbers as before,
For death had thinned their primal ranks
And hunger's pangs oppressed them sore.

A time of peace seemed now at hand
And Aowasting's shores rejoiced,
In song the waters told their joys,
Thro' trees the winds their pæans voiced,
But when the stars of evening came,
A plaintive song stole o'er the wave,
From Dalmaqua, whose heart still mourned
O'er loved Nakosing's sylvan grave.

*Dalmaqua's Requiem at Her Father's Grave*

Shadows of evening, sorrow's sweet mantle,
Spread o'er the earth and soothe it to rest;
Gift of the Manitou, peaceful and gentle,
Heal the deep wounds in my lonely breast;
Hide from the world my grief for my father,
Lest it may sadden those who are brave;
Here in this wild, let me the rather
A requiem sing, all alone, by his grave.

Star of the evening, shining so mildly,
Are you a spirit-land where I shall find
Rest for a weary heart, beating so wildly
While in this lower world sadly confined?
Is there a hunting ground within your border
Where peace and joy shall ever abide?
Freed are its fields from strife and disorder,
Its people from cruelty, avarice, pride?

Cloud of the evening, are you not watching
The spirits of mortals plumed for the sky,
Ready to aid them, eagerly catching
Their notes and songs, as homeward they fly?
Bend to the earth, if such be your mission,
And bear me away to my father's abode;
Such unto me will be happy transition,
Such the escape from life's weary load.

Wind of the evening, spirit of Manitou,
Soft is the voice you bring to my ear;
Sweet are your promises, so kind and true,
Spoken in tones to me gentle and clear.
Waft me away with you to that elysian
Where with my father peace may be mine;
Life to me here seems only a vision
Of storms and sorrows, where suns seldom
    shine.

Voice of the Manitou, in me abiding,
Soothing my soul into sweetest repose,
Sever the bonds so strangely dividing
My spirit-born joys from my incarnate woes.
Then when from bondage free, spirit un-
      fettered,
Songs without sorrow my tongue shall employ,
Then shall my requiems no more be uttered,
But pæans ecstatic, expressive of joy.

### Second Captivity of Petrus Pels

The youthful captive, Petrus Pels,
The maiden's plaintive song had heard,
And knowing cause for which she moaned,
His heart and soul were doubly stirred,
For Evert Pels, his sire, had been
A party in that former strife,
When he whom Dalmaqua now wept,
At Ponckhockie, surrendered life.

'Twas more than sympathy he felt,
'Twas more than pity he bestowed,
A deeper passion burned within,
A tenderness of soul, that glowed
And found expression through an art
Untaught save by the powers above,
Which melt the dross in human heart,
And leave unselfish, holy love.

O holy love! earth's sweetest flower,
Imported here on angel's wing,
Which caught the seed while loitering
Within the garden of the King;
Then hasting earthward in its flight,
Bearing to man the germ of heaven,
Transplanted in the human heart
The fairest flower to mortals given.

Its perfume lifts the saddened soul
And links it to its Sire Divine;
Its fragrance speaks of brotherhood,
Wherein all peoples shall combine;
It knows no color, sect, or race,
As special guardian of its worth,
For He, whose messenger it is,
Has sown it broadcast o'er the earth.

Such flower is but a flame frcm heaven,
An emanation, sweet, divine,
Implanted in the human breast
By God's beneficent design,
To melt the refuse of the heart,
And cast the vicious parts aside,
Retaining atoms which withstand
The flames by which they're purified.

DALMAQUA'S RETREAT, NEAR THE CARVED ROCK

He dwelt in peace her friends among,
He joined in chase, he learned their arts,
He shared their sports, their joys, their woes,
He won his way into their hearts;
And when the sun returning came
From southern skies, whence it had fled,
Around the campfire's evening blaze,
The maiden and the captive wed.

### Their Aowasting Home

Within the rocky clove they dwelt,
Whence Shawangunk's peak leaps nearest
        heaven,
Where cliffs, reflecting rays of sun,
From rocks whose polish had been given
In primal days, when earth was young
And scoured by drifts from Arctic seas;
There sheltered from the tempest rude,
They dwelt 'mong mossy rocks and trees.

When vernal suns the lake had warmed,
And Nature robed herself in green,
When mists at morn and evening hung
O'er woods and vales the cliffs between,
When bird and beast betrayed least fear,
And streams attuned their sweetest song,
Here Dalmaqua in happiness
Dwelt Aowasting's scenes among.

She visited her father's grave
And shed thereon a silent tear;
On Aowasting's crystal wave,
She plied the oar, devoid of fear;
Her songs were changed in word and tone,
Peace smiled benign on every side;
Though present none, seemed not alone,
Her mood bespoke a happy bride.

Here dwelt she had since infancy,
Here witnessed many a joyous feast,
When huntsmen, from successful chase,
Brought home the bird and beast.
Here at the crossing chieftains met
To counsel and prepare for war;
The world had centre here for her,
No land she deemed afar.

Feeling thus that Aowasting
Formed the confines of a sphere,
Wherein all her loves were centred,
Wherein all things seemed most dear,
All her soul burst forth in singing
Pæans of this region wild,
Telling of those charms of Nature,
Sweet and pure to Nature's child.

### *Apostrophe to Aowasting*

Aowasting!  Aowasting!
Place of resting at the crossing,
Where sweet waters, pure and cooling,
Slake the thirst of huntsmen, chasing
Deer and panther in dark forests,
Place of rocks and woods and valleys,
Rugged ledges, dark ravines,
Wherein dwell wild beasts of prey.

Aowasting!  Aowasting!
Place of crossing and of resting,
Where the balsam and the fir tree.
Perfume all the evening air,
Where a fragrance ever hovers
On the buoyant breeze that comes
To assuage fatigue and languor
After chase and toil are done.

Aowasting!  Aowasting!
At the noontide gently basking,
Yields her moisture to the skies
Till the sunset clouds are casting
Heavenly hues far in the west;
Splendor lingers in the distance
Till the changeful rays of evening,
Trembling leave the mountain crest.

Aowasting!   Aowasting!
Place of resting, resting, resting,
Sweet retreat from strife and toil,
Where the sunlight gilds the waters
With a radiance and smile
From the spirit of its Maker,
Fraught with joys perfect and lasting,
Sweet solace for the mind and soul.

Aowasting!   Aowasting!
Wrapped in starlight, moonlight, sunlight,
Censered with balsam and with pine
Swung by magic hand æolian,
Rocked in cradle soft, divine,
Nature's God has crowned you empress
Of this land of peace and rest —
Land of joy in beauty dressed.

Aowasting!   Aowasting!
At your shrine mortals are tasting
Joys akin to heaven alone;
Rarely earth such rest hath known;
Heaven itself seems not far distant,
For the quiet rest you give,
Brings a perfect joy which tells us,
By your shores 'tis bliss to live.

HARVARD LEDGE, OVERLOOKING UNIVERSITY BAY, NEAR OUTLET OF LAKE AOWASTING

Aowasting!  Aowasting!
Nevermore may Peace be hasting,
Swift pursued by Strife and War;
May her reign be everlasting,
On your bright, enchanting shore,
Where my vision eye is chasing
Shadows dear, long gone before,
Of my kindred, here no more.

Aowasting!  Aowasting!
When my soul at its departing
Cleaves its clay, to upward soar,
May a glow of heaven be resting
On your bosom, as of yore
I beheld you in my childhood,
Radiant from shore to shore —
Type of heaven's fair open door.

Beneath the sheltering wings of Peace
Contentment smiled on every hand,
Joy, her attendant, downy clad,
Distilled her blessings o'er the land;
Benignant heaven her fruitage gave,
Obedient to the genial rays
And copious showers and fervid nights,
Essential to the growing maize.

For four short years unbroken Peace
Had reigned on Aowasting's shore;
To Dalmaqua a son was born —
A joy to her unknown before:
That joy supreme a mother feels,
When at the first and feeble cry
Of God-gift to this lower world,
Her soul is filled with ecstasy.

But once again the fires of war
Burn in the valleys round the lake,
And war-whoops through the forests ring,
Calling the wronged their thirst to slake
In blood, unless from foreign seas
Shall be returned captives of war,
Consigned to toil and slavery
On hot Curacoa's isle afar.

The scout and messenger now sought
An audience with those in power,
To avert the sharp, portentous blow
That o'er the future seemed to lower;
The captive whites were all returned
Save Petrus Pels who chose to stay
With Dalmaqua and infant son,
Whom he refuséd to betray.

Petrus Pels, asked to abandon
Wife and child, refused with scorn,
Choosing rather to be faithful
To his wife, and child new-born.
Burned his soul with indignation
At the treacherous wish implied,
And from depths of manly bosom
Thus he to the scouts replied:

### Pels' Reply

"I have heard the plaints and wailings
Of this people wronged by whites,
Forced from home, from field and river,
Robbed by fraud of primal rights,
Maddened by those fiery waters
Unknown ere the white man came,
Slaughtered they have been in riots,
As in forests, slay we game.

"I have seen their hands extended,
Asking justice for their own;
I have seen their pleadings baffled,
All their hopes and joys o'erthrown;
Stricken thus, no hope of justice,
Is it strange they should impinge
On that stubborn gift of Nature,
Born of baffled hopes — Revenge?

"All I am was freely given
Deepest sorrow to assuage,
Sorrow, that no words can utter,
Nor can artist paint a page
Whereon anguish can be portrayed
Such as Dalmaqua has felt,
When in lamentation, sadly
At her father's grave she knelt.

"There I heard her wail of sorrow,
There her requiem for him
Who was slaughtered at Ponckhockie
On that night, when stern and grim,
My own people slew her father
And of his companions, seven,
Whose offense was in partaking
Fiery liquid to them given.

"I will not desert my offspring,
Manhood, I will not desert;
Dalmaqua shall find me faithful,
For to me she gave her heart,
If my life be price for staying,
Scarcely, now, can it atone
For the wrongs my kin inflicted
On this loved one — now my own.

"Ties of kinship are not stronger
Than the ties of Justice, Right;
He who falters at decision,
Wages an unequal fight;
He whose hand defends a brother
Who has outraged Nature's laws,
Soon himself will be a felon,
Else, must bid such action pause.

"Tell my kindred Death can only
Call me from my duty here,
And when he shall send his summons,
My response shall know no fear;
I, to him, will yield compliance
When his messenger shall call,
Whether at the peaceful fireside
Or in battle's carnival.

"Life to me is more than breathing,
More than simply drawing breath,
He who fails to do life's duty
Doubly dies ignoble death.
Let me, when earth's cares are ended,
Know that I have served the right,
Kept the trust to me imparted,
Fought a manlike, noble fight.

"Then when Death shall hover o'er me,
And my spirit wings its flight
To the regions of the unknown,
I will fear no boding night;
I will keep the 'talent' given,
Use it as a true man should,
Bending not to wrong or envy,
Nor to hate's vicissitude."

### Assassination of Petrus Pels

Scarcely had these words been spoken,
When there came, from ambush nigh,
Leaden hail, from cloud whose thunder
Fell not from the upper sky.
Pierced and bleeding was the hero
Who had spoken manly word;
Scout and comrade then departed,
Save by Petrus Pels unheard.

Still he lived to tell the story;
And his faithful Dalmaqua
Nursed him with a hand most tender
On his bed of skins and straw,
Till his strength seemed fast returning
And his eyes were bright and clear;
Then he faded like the twilight,
Leaving darkness dense and drear.

Sorrow seized the widowed mother
With a sharpness like a sword,
Filled her heart with burning anguish
At the death of her loved lord.
Twice her heart had now been riven
By the pale-face who had come
To despoil her fields and forests
And deprive her of her home.

Devoid of Hope, of Peace deprived,
Flung helpless on life's murky sea
Whose windward waves leap mountain high
And leeward roar sounds threateningly,
Whose giant jaws, with white foam bathed,
Stand wide ajar, prone to devour,
While angry skies wild lightnings flash,
And drifting clouds destruction lower,

The human heart recoils in fear,
And fancy's wings are shorn of flight;
Else, bathed in darkness more intense
Than moonless, starless, cheerless night;
Then self alone too weak will prove,
Too transient every self-born aid;
A Father's hand the storm can quell,
And leave the soul, calm, undismayed.

Full fifty moons had waxed and waned,
Four harvests fallen to decay;
A hundred sheets of downy white
Had fallen on the frozen bay;
Four times the sun had climbed the sky
And then returnéd whence he came;
The autumn chase four times had drawn
The huntsmen to their feasts of game;

Four times with leaves the trees were decked,
Then fallen, rustled to the wind;
The wild flowers on the hills and shores
Four times had left their joys behind,
Since Petrus Pels, the captive, came
To share this joyous lake and land,
To win the hearts of warriors brave
And orphaned Dalmaqua's loved hand.

Twice the death-blow sharp had fallen
On the idols of her heart;
Only one — her son — now lingered;
All too soon might she depart;
How she planned true worth to teach him —
A father's only legacy —
May be learned by closely scanning
This her brief soliloquy:

The flint-wrought face of Petrus Pels,
As carved by faithful Dalmaqua,
Upon the granite block which tells
Her soul's devotion to that law
Which binds affianced hearts in one,
By silken cords that will not quail,
Nor let the bondage be undone,
When storms and tempests fierce assail.

At Aowasting Lake, near Minnewaska Lake, Shawangunk
Mountains, New York.   (From photograph.)

"For him, the pale-faced chief I wed,
Who fell defending me and him
Who bears his image as his son,
I daily chant a requiem.
Lest his dear image shall depart
And fade from memory's feeble throne,
His perfect face let me here carve
Upon the tablet of this stone.

"With skill directed by that hand
Which never errs, but perfect is,
The hand which soothes a heart oppressed
And holds life's deepest mysteries.
Mine be the purpose, His the skill,
To carve each feature true and grand
Upon this granite block, so well,
Through untold ages it shall stand.

"Here by this rock my joy shall be
Until my work is fully done,
And let his flint-wrought features grow
In sight of his half-orphaned son,
That he, in future years may know
His deeds of valor in defense
Of home, of mother, and of son,
And all its fatal consequence,"

Just below the spring, deep hidden
In the crevice of the clove,
Where the rugged rocks lie broken,
Hurled from towering cliffs above,
Are those features carved in fullness
By the hand that eased his pain,
When, refusing to desert her,
He in treachery was slain.

There for many months she labored
With her flinty chisel strong,
Cheered by none save him she cherished
As sole solace for her wrong;
Day by day she told the story
Of a father's loving heart;
Moulded she the father's image,
Not alone in sculptured art.

As those features grew in beauty
On the granite stone she cut,
Till the perfect face was shapen
And the rock seemed lifeless not,
All her soul was merged in patience,
Scanning every point and pose,
Perfect were the eyes and forehead,
Cheek and chin, and lips and nose.

Age on age has wrought great changes,
Yet that facial form appears
Scarcely marred by Time's fell ravage
Of two hundred fifty years.
There it stands, still looking southward,
Crown still resting on its head,
Like a sentinel there guarding
The heroic, faithful dead.

Fancy feigns that tears are falling
From the sunken, moss-dimmed eye,
While the knitted, wrinkled forehead,
Half suggests a pang-born sigh;
But the mouth of Titan firmness,
And the bearded chin so strong,
Both proclaim such fancied weakness,
Does the sphinx-like statue wrong.

Here 'mid rocks, in wild confusion,
Cast from cliffs by Nature's laws,
Lifting high its massive figure,
'Mid the mountains' giant jaws,
Rests the sculptured face of Petrus,
Scarcely marred by break or flaw,
Wrought by hand, divinely tutored,
Of the faithful Dalmaqua.

Here for ages shall those features
Tell the story of her wrongs,
Still she lives in lake and legend,
Though long since have died her songs.
Father, husband, son, and mother,
All the numerous tribal train,
Now have found their sweet elysian,
But those features still remain.

He who aids a fallen brother
On his way to honor's goal,
Builds within himself a fortress,
Staunch and stable, for his soul;
Sees the world with beauty brighten;
Hears a minstrelsy his own;
Reaps a harvest of contentment
Unto Avarice unknown.

Who from fancied heights may revel
In his vain imagining,
That o'er brothers weak or simple,
God has made him judge or king,
Should remember that as keeper,
He must give unselfish guard,
If he, in the great hereafter,
Would receive a sweet reward.

Save to serve detained dependents
Who may need a helping hand;
Save to succor loved attendants
On their way to Stygian strand;
Save to strew upon life's morrow
Seeds of kindness, deeds of cheer,
Thus allaying pangs of sorrow,
Who would wish to tarry here?

Altruistic love is boundless;
Wide as the ethereal dome;
Compasses God's every creature
That can cheer and bless man's home;
Feeds upon the sweetest impulse
That expands the germ of Truth;
Grows by usage till it covers
Palace grand and lowly booth;

Sings its song in treble measure,
Tuned to sea and land and sky;
Hails with joy repentant brother
Whom all others would decry;
Sees in the *beyond* a beauty
Purer than the vile can see;
Lifts the veil that hides the Father
From the soul's sincerity;

Builds on Faith and Works foundation
For a home pure, undefiled,
Whose enchantments and estrangements
Shall be fully reconciled,
After transit from its mundane
To its heavenly abode,
And aside is laid love human
For the perfect love of God.

When the mists within the valley,
Which like billowy oceans seem,
Shall be touched by light from heaven,
And God's radiance shall gleam
Through the darkness, thus dispelling
All the gloom and woe and wrong,
Changed may be the wail of sorrow
Into a triumphant song.

When with pomp and glow and splendor,
Man has builded for himself,
On the wrecks of fellow creatures,
Castles stained with blood and pelf,
Wrung from brothers whose vain pleading
Brought no sympathizing word,
Can he in the final judgment
Hope to meet a smiling Lord?

When the trump of the archangel
Summons earth her dead to yield
Then the secrets of life's action
Can no longer be concealed.
When the earth shall melt and crumble
At the Master's great command,
Rock and figure, lake and mountain,
Shall as mentors no more stand.

Truthful words shall then be spoken,
Silent tongues shall secrets tell,
Adamantine hearts shall soften,
Penance pearls from eyes shall well,
When the Master sends the summons
That admits of no evade,
And the victor and his victim
Each in Truth shall be arrayed.

Happy he who sees as brother
Each and all of human form;
Sees as links in chain of Nature
Godlike man and lowly worm;
Sees and feels in life's stern conflict
Beast and bird, as well as man,
Have, by Nature, rights inherent,
All decreed by God's own plan.

Petrus, Dalmaqua, and Chambers,
Kieft, Ondoris, white and red —
All shall meet in the hereafter
When the earth shall yield her dead;
Each shall stand before the Master,
As coequal in His sight,
And receive the scourge or honor
Merited for wrong or right.

Wait we must the final judgment
From a just, unerring bar,
To decide if in the balance
All things right adjusted were;
Weights that we compute of value,
By our own imperfect sense,
May be deemed by God unworthy
And of little consequence.

If the lamp God gave to guide us
Has been cherished, burnished, trimmed,
And the light from its Great Maker
Never quenched, never dimmed,
We may trust our faith and labor
And the Wondrous Gift He gave,
Wrap Death's cerements fondly 'round us,
March serenely to the grave.

Lightning Source UK Ltd.
Milton Keynes UK
UKHW02n0830190818
327370UK00002B/16/P